LET THE SUNSHINE IN

By James Alexander Thom

THE C. R. GIBSON COMPANY, PUBLISHERS
NORWALK, CONNECTICUT

FOREWORD

Two things seem scarce in our century: time and worthy thoughts.

We are hurried. We are busy from morning to evening with details, with the busy work of earning our living and keeping our affairs in order. Our precious hours are nibbled away by trivial but complex and necessary concerns.

What time we do have left for our deeper selves? Little indeed. Little time for great books of thought, little time for the discussion of exciting ideals, for meditation and loving-kindness, for the sort of things that stretch our minds and enrich our souls.

We lament the flight of spiritual values from our lives. But, really, how much attention do we give to these values: to integrity, courage, humanism, honor? So very little; we're too busy with details.

This book was written precisely because of that scarcity of time and worthy thoughts. I believe that we must insert, here and there among the petty details of our existence, some basic considerations about the purposes, the meanings, the satisfactions of life.

I do not presume that any busy person would want to spend much time reading my words. Therefore, I have made each essay and story quite brief. It is the kind of material a modern person can read in one- and two-minute interludes between his many necessary tasks. What these pieces lack in length, I believe, they compensate for in significance and good humor. They are the important things of life, put in nutshells, for your mind to snack into convenient moments — and then to ruminate on.

Pleasant reading!

— James Alexander Thom

CHAPTER I
HAPPINESS

HAPPINESS IS INTENTIONAL

THERE'S been a staggering lot of sense and nonsense written, spoken, and sung about how to be happy — and about whether happiness is even possible. Philosophers, poets, and preachers can take most of the theories about happiness and make them mean what they will. A poet might tell us to pursue happiness, while a philosopher will tell us that to pursue it is the quickest way to lose it. A preacher might tell us that the only happiness is in the meekness of the lamb; a philosopher might tell us that happiness is the feeling of power increasing.

The things that have been said about happiness would fill libraries; the things left *unsaid* about happiness would scarcely crowd a greeting card.

Yet in all this literature, discourse, and song about happiness, we have seen only one or two plain, practical, incontrovertibly true statements. And the first one that comes to mind is the one by America's own wizard of commonsense, Abraham Lincoln, who said that: "*Most folks are about as happy as they make up their minds to be.*"

Reflect on that one for a moment. Think about it in terms of the various jolly or misanthropic persons you know. Think what you've heard various optimists or pessimists, rich people or poor people, say about happiness. Better yet, try to remember whether you yourself have ever declared, "By gosh, life *is* good, and I know it is, and I can be happy in it, happy with whatever comes my way."

If you have never issued yourself that ultimatum, you might try it and see if it works, even just a little.

Most of us know some grouchy, cynical malcontent who spreads inky gloom wherever he goes; we knew one of whom it was said, "He goes into a room, and turns everybody off." These glum souls insist that life is but one long keelhauling, and humanity is but a basket of asps. These are persons who have made up their minds that they're going to be *unhappy*, come what may; and they almost succeed. We say "almost" because, ironically, they get so satisfied with the misery they've created for themselves that they're *happy* with that, thus defeating their end. But, we suppose, if they're unhappy to learn that they're actually happy with their unhappiness, then they're nice and unhappy again, and that ought to make them happy. (You see how hard it is to say anything absolute about happiness?)

At any rate, if people like that can make up their minds they're going to be unhappy, and then do so well at it, doesn't it seem logical that others can similarly make up their minds to be happy, as Lincoln said, and then *be* that happy?

Of course Lincoln didn't mean such people would spend the rest of their lives chasing happiness like a rainbow. He just meant they'll *intend* to be happy, and then go on happily about their business.

WHO'S HAPPY?

SOME years ago, a London newspaper offered prizes for the best answers to this question: "Who are the happiest persons on earth?" The answers were so surprising and encouraging that we like to think of them occasionally. Here are the four answers adjudged the best:

"A craftsman or artist whistling over a job well done."

"A little child building sand castles."

"A mother, after a busy day, bathing her baby."

"A doctor who has finished a difficult and dangerous operation, and saved a human life."

What? No playboys? No millionaires? No international jet-setters? No kings? No Hollywood idols? No addicts high on drugs? It looks as if kicks, riches, fame, and rank are not rated as highly as essentials of a happy life. Plainly the decision is that happiness is for everybody, not for just a privileged few. If no one but the glamorous and the rich could be happy, then the rest of us might have real grounds for complaint.

But happily, that doesn't seem to be the case, does it?

SIMPLIFY YOUR LIFE

A MAN (and this goes for women as well) has happiness almost in the palm of his hand if he can fill his days with real work and his nights with real rest. Unhappiness grows when his work and his rest are not real — when he is distracted, detained, or prevented from accomplishing his tasks fully, or when his rest is nibbled away by aimless chores, disorder, and worry. These things — the pointless distractions, the little fears and confusions — gnaw away his contentment like foraging rodents in a granary.

If a man would promote his own happiness, then let him start a crash program to simplify his life. Let him analyze his work tasks and give priority to the essential ones; then let him round up all the meaningless and bothersome influences in his private life and rush them out of the house once and for all.

Perhaps the best advice on living we've ever heard was Thoreau's one-word dictum: "*Simplify!*" Let a man trim all the fat off his life, let him reduce his hours down to lean purposes and rewards, and there he may stand — smiling — with the chance for real work, real rest, and probably real happiness, right in his hand.

BEING WELL-WED

PERHAPS it is time for a good word or two about marriage. We don't hear *good words* about marriage very often anymore, except from marryin' preachers or marriage counselors. Almost everybody else considers the subject a target for wisecracks, gibes, and cynicism. The folks who have discovered the profound joys of good marriage aren't often heard from; perhaps if they were, the whole institution would regain some of its prestige.

Lately, the freedom and irresponsibility of bachelorhood (male and female) have been lauded; the great heroes in the eyes of the foolish and frivolous these days are the super-bachelors of the jet set, with their temporary and hedonistic sexual alliances. But their pleasures are fleeting; let's forget about them and think for a moment on what a good marriage is and why it is such a lasting blessing.

All other advantages aside, it might be said that the greatest thing a good marriage does for a person is this: *it gives him another soul besides his own to love permanently.* (Of course, as the critics of marriage say, it also gives him another complex soul besides his own to *contend* with permanently, but there's plenty of room for contention within love.) Anyway, having another soul to love is the greatest thing that can happen to a person. Before this, all the walls of his soul are covered with mirrors and he sees only himself — always.

But the love of another's soul puts doors and windows in those walls, and he can escape from the confinement of his self. It takes maturity, of course, and a great deal of understanding for one to appreciate this freedom from self. Indeed, many married persons never do understand it; theirs are the marriages that go bad. Those who do understand it, though . . . well look at them — and you'll see what happiness is all about.

GIVING TO GET

FOR everything we gain, we have to sacrifice something. Nothing's free. We all know that, deep in our hearts. But knowing it down deep sometimes isn't enough as we go along from day to day; it's necessary that we keep reminding ourselves of the rule.

If we don't keep in mind that we have to give to get, we're constantly being disappointed to discover that we have to pay for some advantage or other.

We want freedom. Then we learn that we've got to pay for it with diligence and participation.

We want wealth or prestige. Then we learn that we've got to devote a great deal of our time and effort to attaining them. If we want to be famous, we'll have to sacrifice privacy.

We want conveniences and labor-saving devices. Then we learn that we've got to pay for them in money and care.

We want to be trusted, but learn that we've got to earn it by being trustworthy ourselves.

We want to receive love, but discover that we've got to give of our own loving. We want peace of mind, but learn that we won't have it if we rob others of *their* peace of mind.

We want pleasure, but have to remember that there can be costly consequences and responsibilities following up pleasure.

If we want to be educated, we have to study. If we want to be healthy and strong, we have to follow rules of hygiene and exercise to build up our bodies. If we want to accomplish something, we have to discipline ourselves to stick to the task, even when we're exhausted and discouraged.

Sorry, that's just the way it is. That's the rule. But if we get it integrated into our thinking, then we won't go around having vain expectations of windfalls and unearned prizes. And if we don't have those foolish hopes, we'll have fewer disappointments.

The big bonus to this reality is, of course, that when we do pay for what we get, then we not only have what we've gotten, but we also have the satisfaction of having gotten it in the right and real way — a satisfaction that we wouldn't have had if everything had just fallen in our laps.

11

"HAPPINESS IS . . ."

GOING the rounds these days is the uncompleted phrase, "Happiness is . . ." It is up to the individual to put in the word or words that will complete the phrase to suit his particular notion of what happiness is.

The phrase shows that happiness is a very personal and subjective thing; no two persons are likely to define it the same way.

There is also some evidence that a person's idea of happiness is more likely to be based on something he wants than on something he has. We are reminded of what Charles Elliott said in *Gone Fishin'*:

"Every gesture we make in life is either a firm or a faltering step toward happiness, something we interpret in terms of what we do not have. Those of us who are poor in material things seek wealth. The sick know that happiness lies in health, the lonely want companionship, the harassed are eternally seeking the solitude of seclusion. Happiness is interpreted always in terms of things we do not have."

A good observation, that. Although we may not agree with him on the word "always," we'll have to admit that this usually is the case. Few persons would finish the "Happiness is . . ." phrase with "everything staying just as it is now for me."

But if we should hear somebody answer that way, probably we should congratulate him on being a fortunate and well-adjusted man — and a rare one at that.

PURPOSE

BLESSED is he who has a good purpose. Accursed is he who has none. So simply can the eternal question of happiness in life be answered. Men seek happiness in bizarre and complicated ways, and most despair of ever finding it. Yet, there it is, in the simplest and most obvious formula: happiness is in a good purpose.

Do you doubt this? If you do, then research it in your own soul. Probe for it in your own memory. What does it please you most to remember? Think back for a moment. What was your pleasantest time?

Surely it was a time when you were striving for something — not something you specifically called by the name of happiness — but some other specific thing which seemed important and worthwhile.

12

Was it when you were studying to learn a useful trade? Very likely. Was it when you were trying to please someone? Your parents, perhaps, or your mate? Quite probably. Was it when you were sacrificing long hours to serve some cause you fervently believed in? Conceivably, it was then. Was it when you were trying to impart some ideals, some decency, some nobility to your children? Surely it was then.

Those good times were when you were striving for something worthwhile, then, were they not? And now, notice something else about those efforts. There is something they all have in common:

They were being done not primarily for yourself, not primarily for your own happiness — but for someone else.

That, finally, is our definition of a good purpose: something outside the self, needing to be done.

This is a curious fact, and it takes most of us a long time to discover it — if, indeed, we ever do. Happiness, that long-shot human goal, is not in getting, but in giving. It sounds odd: you keep on taking until you end up with nothing that's worth having. But you keep on giving, and you end up with everything that's worth having.

Anyone who's still not convinced will just have to try it himself.

CHAPTER II
PERCEPTION

OUR MENTAL TELESCOPE

SO MANY people carry around with them a telescope that they don't know how to use. Not a real, solid telescope with glass lenses, but a mental one.

Many telescopes have a small lens in one end and a large lens in the other. When we put the small lens against the eye and look through, the things we see appear enlarged. But when we put the large lens against the eye, the things we're looking at appear reduced, tiny in size.

Our mental telescope works the same way, and it seems that many people go around looking at things wrongly through it — looking through the wrong end at the wrong time. Here are some examples.

When we look at other people's mistakes, we put the little end of the telescope to our eye and magnify the mistakes greatly. But when we look at our own mistakes, we point the little end at them and make them look as tiny and insignificant as possible.

When we look at problems, we do it the other way around: we point the big lens at our own problems, magnifying them, but aim the little lens at others' problems, making them look tiny and minor. The same goes for the few good deeds we do: we magnify them. But the good deeds others do for us, well, often we reduce them to a minimum. And usually look at our rights v. the rights of others in this same way.

Too many of us also look at the basic values and purposes of our lives with the telescope turned wrong-end to. Don't we, too often, aim that big end of the telescope toward such things as status symbols, wealth, luxury, thrills of the moment, security, and ease, magnifying them far above their real importance? And

15

don't we aim that little end toward ideals, toward the attainment of wisdom, toward beauty, toward human dignity, toward the true meanings of life?

We have all seen persons who will keep the magnifying end of the mental telescope trained on a big car, a big deal, a juicy pleasure, or the key to the executive washroom, but always look the other way through it at God or their fellow man.

Let us then, learn how to use this mental telescope of ours correctly. Let us try to keep the magnifying end sighted on worthy things and on selfless things. And if we must look at the trivial and selfish things at all, let's focus on them with the reducing lens.

LET THE SUNSHINE IN

WE SOMETIMES speak of rays of sunshine as if they were symbolic of happiness. A grandparent, doting on a granddaughter, may call the child "a little ray of sunshine." (A good moment at the end of a hard day comes "like a ray of sunshine.")

We may not realize just how apt those words are until we think what makes a ray of sunshine. It is not just the sun itself shining. On a brilliant, cloudless day, on a plain or on the sea, there are no rays of sunshine to be seen. There may be a brilliant flood of sunlight, yes, but no rays.

We see rays of sunshine — sunbeams — only when the sunlight is shining through a gap in something darker or something solid. We see sunbeams leaning down to earth through a rift in dark clouds. We see sunbeams slanting through windows into a shadowy room. We see sunshine as rays in a forest where it comes through the dark leaves and dapples the ground with light. Or when it filters through thick mist or smoke. In other words, it is the contrasting darkness or the partial blocking of sunlight that makes rays of the sun.

In the same way, it is the surrounding shadow of trouble or sorrow that makes happiness glow like a sunbeam when it does come through. Just as there are no noticeable sunbeams on a

16

cloudless day, so would happiness be unfelt in a totally untroubled life. It is the contrast, the relief, that makes happiness distinctive. As Henry Wadsworth Longfellow said: "The rays of happiness, like those of light, are colorless when unbroken."

THE ART OF SELECTIVE LOOKING

THERE'S an old maxim which says that people often cannot see the forest for the trees, meaning they concentrate so much on single facts, they can't comprehend the larger scheme of things.

But maybe it's time someone turned that old saying around to remind us that sometimes we can't see the trees for the forest. These days, such crowded panoramas pass before our eyes that it is hard to get a meaningful glimpse of any single thing.

Perhaps we should practice the art of selective looking once in a while and try to see the *trees* instead of the forest.

Certainly, there is something to be said for this selective looking. Scientists do it and achieve great things. Artists do it and achieve beautiful things. The scientist, in his research, focuses on some specific thing, like the nature of a virus or the structure of an atom, and if he finally understands it, he can use that understanding as the key to a broader understanding of disease or of matter.

The artist looks selectively for the basic line, form, or hue which makes something in life beautiful. Finding it, he puts it down clearly so people may see it and understand a little more about beauty, or even about life itself. He is, like the scientist, looking for the key.

If we do not stop and consider the meaning of a tree, then to us the forest will be no more than a green-brown bristle on the earth's face. But if we do understand the tree, we will know that the forest enriches the air with oxygen, cools the breezes, harbors animal life, holds and fertilizes the soil, helps keep nature in its essential balance, and even performs such little side favors as inspiring poets and enchanting lovers.

In the same way, if one never stops to consider his own true motives for the things he does, then to him all other people's actions will be aimless and suspect. But if he does try to understand himself, then he will have the key to knowing what people want, why they work, why they help or hurt each other, how he can get them to do things for him and how he can do things for them.

One of the best-known current American slogans is "Think Big." It is a good slogan, tersely telling us to try to fit things into the overall scheme, to see the forest and not get hung up on any little tree.

Even so, it seems reasonable to say that if you can't understand one thing, you shouldn't expect to understand everything.

LOOK AT AN OLD FACE

LOOK at an old face. Then, instead of looking on past it and forgetting it, look at it a bit longer and ponder on what that face might have faced in its time. How many world wars has it gazed on with worried brow? Has it been lighted by the flare of artillery, or shadowed by the smoke of fires in rubble? Has it been chapped by cold and wind? Has it grimaced against mustard gas or wept at the sight of fallen comrades?

Has that face perhaps seen depression years wear by, its eyes searching for what might be the next odd job, the next plain meal? Has that face brooded over menial work and sagged with drudgery that seemed unending?

Has that face presided over the comings of offspring and the passing of friends and relatives? Has it outlasted most of the faces it used to look upon with affection?

Has it survived the constant sacrifice and compromise of a long, long marriage? Has it seen in twenty thousand morning mirrors the relentless vanishing of its youth?

The next time you look upon an old face, don't merely look past and go on. Wonder about the dreams that face has masked. What had that person intended to be? A strong and handsome leader? An inventor? A prize winning scientist? A famous actress, an author, a mother of presidents? Certainly there were dreams of everything but becoming an old man or woman.

On what particular day did that person wake up realizing that the great dreams were no longer there, that it was just too late? When did that person admit that he or she had traded in all the ideals and glorious plans for a few more years of survival? When did that face lose the grin of passion and assume the small smile of content?

When did that face finally face the great lesson of resignation? How many times has the soul behind that face been in and out of faith and doubt? How many times has it given up and how many times has it started over?

Look at the wrinkles in that old face. Do they sag with accrued frowning, or tilt up from the laughing habit? Are there scars or lines of pain from once-dread illnesses?

Well, when you look into a face like that, don't expect it to look back at you in envy of your youth. Don't expect it to regret the long, long line of yesterdays.

Perhaps the thousands of days and scores of years that face has faced have been hard ones, worse than you would care to anticipate. But just ask that person about those struggling times. And likely that old face will crinkle with smiles and that old voice will say: "Ah, those were the good old days."

TRAPPING TRUTH IN A PRISM

IT MIGHT help us to make better judgments if we think of truth as being trapped inside a prism. What we mean is this: any personality, any doctrine, any event or any philosophy can look entirely different when seen from different sides. The basic truth of it is in there, but in order to see the real shape and dimension of the truth, it is necessary to turn the prism this way and that. It is necessary to look carefully in through each of the facets — because the truth will look slightly distorted, one way or another, in any single one of the facets.

One of the best examples of the many-sidedness of any truth is an automobile collision seen by three or four witnesses. Each may swear that he saw exactly what happened, yet each one's story is likely to differ from the others', and the drivers' stories may be still different. So the police officer investigating the accident has to write down each witness' story, and then do a lot of checking and deducing of his own — measuring and noting the direction of skid marks, the pattern of fallen debris, and so forth.

Another good example is when two persons discuss a mutual acquaintance; their impressions might be so diverse that one would presume they were talking about two different persons. Actually, they've just been shown different sides of that person, and have subjectively interpreted what they have been shown.

On anything from a family squabble to a public issue, then, it should be obvious that the prism will have many facets. It would be sheer stupidity to look at such an issue only through the facet that's nearest you, imagining that you're seeing the whole truth in its real form. Yet, that is what most of us habitually do. We look at a controversy, or evaluate a personage, only through the nearest facet; that is, through our accustomed points of view, our preconceptions, our prejudices. That's the only way we look at it; there we get a grossly erroneous and probably oversimplified version of the truth. It's the lazy way to arrive at conclusions, and the irresponsible way.

Doubtless many of the troubles in this world could be solved if people would take the time to look for the truth as if it were in a prism.

THE SMALL VIEW

ONE winter day, when the trees were bare of leaves and heavy clouds kept sunlight from illuminating the earth, we put on our heavy coats and went out to walk in the countryside. It was a section of land we had always loved to see in spring, summer, and fall, when flowers and foliage were rich and the views were vast and colorful and charged with sunlight.

This winter day, however, we did not expect to see much beauty; we just wanted the exercise of a brisk walk in the cold air. But we were no sooner out on this bleak landscape than we did begin noticing things that were exquisitely beautiful. Little things they were, like the lacework of ice forming on wet soil; fallen red oak leaves seeming brighter because of the grayness around them; the graceful tracery of bare branches; the silvery fluff of certain dry weed-flowers swaying in the wind on the hillsides; and subtle colors of mosses and lichens on the rocks underfoot. There was also the mute marvel of a rock split by a growing tree; the velvety light blue of juniper berries and the reds of bittersweet and sumac; and the deep violet hue of distant slopes.

These were things too low-key to have been seen when we were drunk with the riots of color in the other seasons, too subtle and small to show in competition with flowers and greenery. Yet somehow, these small wintry wonders told us more about life's miracle than we could comprehend. It was a reverent excitement we felt on that winter day.

CHAPTER III
TREATMENT
OF OURSELVES

MAKING WAVES

WHEN someone wants to maintain the *status quo*, he warns, "*Don't make waves!*" You've heard the expression. The "*waves*," of course, are change.

Lots of waves are being stirred up these days. The trouble is that most people are upset by change; they resent it, they fear it, they go along grumbling, and resisting the change. (Not that they were all that happy with the way things were; they grumbled about that too. But it was more comfortable and secure than new and relentless waves of change.)

Let us learn a lesson from the surfboarder. He has a passion for ocean waves. He studies them, anticipates them. He learns how they behave, how they can carry him farthest and give him the most exhilarating ride. The surfer thus becomes a scientist of waves, an artist of wave-riding, trying to stay always just before the breaking crest. And if he's dumped, he plunges back into the water, his ability nevertheless reinforced by the experience.

We should all learn to ride the waves of change that way.

YOU'RE ONE OF A KIND

REST happy in the knowledge that there's no one quite like you. In this whole world there's nobody else exactly like you, which is another way of saying that probably in the whole universe you are an exclusive creation. Regardless of what the computer punch cards and the television rating polls may imply, you aren't just a number like any other number: you are, cell for cell, one of a kind. When they made you, they broke the mold. There's no duplicate of you anywhere, and you've got fingerprints to prove it.

Oh, sure, you may be just as anonymous as a billion others. You may be no better than the rest of them; maybe you're even worse than most. The point is that you can *think* you're better, because you're you.

You've got a name. Maybe no one outside your own family and the place where you work would recognize it, but it's your own name. And it's not like a brand name on a bunch of identical products, either. You may even be one of several thousand Joe Smiths, but you didn't come off an assembly line looking just like those other Joe Smiths. No, sir. You are the one and only Joe Smith, right smack dab in the center of your own particular universe.

Nobody else has exactly the same thoughts you have (at least not in the same order); nobody else has the same dreams you have; nobody else has the same scars you have, and certainly no one else has quite the same history.

No, let's face it. You're just YOU-nique!

(But it's also important to remember that everybody else is just as unique as you are.)

MENTAL CORROSION

DRIP . . . drip . . . drip . . . goes the familiar, irritating sound of water from a leaky faucet at night. As the minutes and hours wear on, it becomes louder. After a while you find yourself absolutely unable to think of anything but that maddening drip . . . drip . . . drip . . .

Ever think how similiar a worry is to a leaky faucet? Like a leaky faucet, a worry usually is a very small and unimportant thing. But it gets bigger and bigger, then all out of proportion, simply because it persists. That little worry gets to the point where it can be the biggest and worst thing in your life.

Another thing a faucet leak does: it corrodes. It gradually wears a channel in the metal or the washer until more and more water can leak out. First a drip, then a dribble, then a trickle, until it's corroded a clear watercourse for itself and it just runs.

So it is with a worry. It corrodes the mind, cutting a channel for itself until it just runs constantly and pretty soon carries all your constructive thought with it. Before long you can't do a good day's work because all your faculties are constantly running toward that channel.

If a worry is that much like a leaky faucet, shouldn't you remedy it the way you remedy a leaky faucet? Doesn't that sound logical? Shouldn't you, instead of lying awake all night cursing that dripping, take your wrench and a new washer and get right into the heart of that faucet and repair the flaw? Likewise, shouldn't you, instead of frowning and fretting and cursing that worry, get right to the heart of it and correct the thing you're worrying about? It'll save you a lot of mental corrosion.

SELF-IMPORTANCE

ANY MAN, no matter how wise, feels that he is the center of everything. He perceives the universe lying in all directions outward from him. He really cannot imagine time before he appeared on the earth, or that time will continue after he has been here. He feels that no happening was ever important until it happened to him. "No one ever felt like this," he cries when he is very miserable, as well as when he is very happy. "No one ever was so clever," he congratulates himself when he has thought something out well.

Because he is within himself looking out, he can feel that no one else among the billions of human beings on earth has any purpose so great as his own. He can, of course, reason that "I am only one more among multitudes," but if he is going to strive for personal achievement, he has to feel certain in his heart that he is someone special.

But the most significant thing about self-importance is that it can be such a great enemy. And without great enemies, we could have no great victories.

When men do rise above their selves, it is said to be their greatest achievement. When they take this all-important thing,

the self, and hand it whole into the keeping of someone else —
friend, mate, mankind or, above all, their God — it is then that
they have their most important victories.

It is when he yields up his self-importance that a man becomes
a truly important self, say the philosophers and the prophets.

"A man becomes extraordinary when he stops thinking he
is unique.

"A man becomes unique when he stops thinking he is extraordinary."

YOU ARE WHAT YOU THINK

THERE'S no escaping the fact that what you are is determined by
what goes on between your ears. You are the manifestation of
your thoughts. Does that scare you? Some of us it could scare
pretty badly. Those of us whose thoughts are petty, cowardly,
lazy, nasty, gloomy, sloppy, and ignoble ought to realize that our
personal traits will be the same. We ought to look into our
thoughts occasionally to see what we're really like. We are not
what we say we are. We are not what other people think we are.
We are what we think.

But this isn't a horrible fact. It's a wonderful fact. Because if
we can shape our thinking for the better, that means we can
shape ourselves for the better. We can get in the habit of thinking
positively, eagerly, industriously, charitably, brightly, bravely,
and nobly. And thus we can make ourselves more positive,
eager, industrious, charitable, bright, brave, and noble, because
we are what we think.

So what do you want to be?

What do you *think* you want to be?

SERENDIPITY

ONE DAY a young businessman had to go up to the store for
some small item that had been forgotten during the regular

shopping. He decided to get the old bicycle out of the garage and pedal up there, instead of starting up the family car. So he wiped the cobwebs off the handlebars, swung astride, and leisurely set out along the roadside.

Just as he got about halfway to the store, a sudden summer rain came up. Since it wasn't an electrical storm, he just drew up under the densely-leafed branches of a roadside maple and decided to wait it out. Now here he was for the first time in many weeks, with nothing to do for the moment, nothing to read, no one to talk to. People, dry in their cars, went on by in the rain, not stranded, just completely unaffected by the weather — the way he usually was.

So the man sat there on his bicycle, filled up his pipe, turned it upside down so that no wayward raindrops making their way through the foliage would extinguish it, and waited. Some people on their porch nearby called out, inviting him to take refuge on the porch, but he smilingly declined. It rained. The air began to smell deliciously cool and clean. The sound of the rain in the leaves was very soothing, blotting out time and the noises of the city. The rain hissing on the wet street made millions of tiny white rain splashes, and little rivulets began to creep across the dry pavement near his bicycle, washing dead grass and gum wrappers into the gutters, and soon a gurgling stream was running along the curb.

After perhaps half an hour of this sweet calm, the clouds moved on and the sun came out, flashing off the puddles and glinting on the wet leaves. Soon our rider went on, reluctantly leaving that spot where he had been caught. He felt very good. He had enjoyed this enforced pause much more than he had enjoyed any planned activity for months.

The ability to find such unsought pleasures is called *serendipity* (after Walpole's *Three Princes of Serendip*, who had this faculty). A degree of serendipity makes life a joy.

But how often, in this hurried modern world of ours, do we allow ourselves to get caught in the rain? How often do we allow ourselves to strike up a rewarding conversation with a complete stranger? How often do we (since boyhood, anyway) stop and skip

27

rocks on the water? How often do we stop in the middle of our planned activities to give somebody a hand?

Not often. We seem to plan our time to avoid serendipitous events, to insulate ourselves against surprises.

Perhaps we shouldn't. For a serendipitous moment is like a good, brief poem — beautiful, meaningful, and memorable.

MAINTENANCE FOR THE HUMAN CHASSIS

ALTHOUGH some might argue the point, the human being is probably still more important than the automobile. Even so, it seems to be much easier to impress a man with the importance of maintaining his car well than himself. Perhaps if we could put man's personal upkeep in automotive terms, might he not do better at keeping himself off the scrap heap? Let's see:

1. The Engine. The engine in the human chassis consists mainly of the device called the "heart." This is a delicately engineered mechanism which, if properly serviced and not abused, ought to provide satisfactory power for 100 years or more. However, it can develop valve fouling, pumpage failure, timing difficulties, and other malfunctions if not kept in proper tune. Excessive idling, too rich fuel mixture, and so forth can cause stiffness, deposits, or parts wear. When the engine gets in this condition, one unaccustomed drag-race can knock it out. Repairs are costly and often impossible. Heart mechanics recently have been experimenting with used-engine swaps — with little success. Borrowed engines somehow seem incompatible in strange vehicles. Use the engine moderately at most times and take it to the shop for annual inspection, and it can continue to give amazing performance.

2. The Air Filter System. In the human vehicle this is known as the "lungs." They are two of the worst-abused components. Unfortunately, mechanics and engineers have developed no known way to change filters, so it becomes increasingly difficult to keep them clean, due to increased traffic exhaust, smoke, and other pollutants. Good maintenance consists primarily of

deep, regular, vigorous use, and keeping smoke intake at a minimum.

3. The Electrical System. In the human chassis, this is known as the "nerves." It is extremely complex, and, because of the great loads placed on it in modern society, has been known to "blow." All the vehicle's accessories and optional luxury equipment operate on this system. The secret of good nerve maintenance seems to be in not using all accessories at once. Do not overload the electrical system; give the battery sufficient rest; and keep close watch on the condition of the Generator. (This is found well forward under the hood and is commonly called the "brain.")

4. Fuel. Customarily, the misuse of fuel ("food" and "drink") in the human vehicle is the most careless and extreme abuse of the machine. Most users tend toward fuel mixes which are too rich and have too many additives, resulting in great fuel waste, bad combustion, sluggish operation, and a condition known as obesity throughout the system. In addition, many use indiscriminately a high-octane fuel ("booze") which often is too powerful for their inadequate combustion and steering systems. Advice: be moderate in the use of "ethyl"; use a fuel mixture that is not too rich or too lean; don't overfill the tank; ideal mpg will result.

General Note: Travel with caution and courtesy to avoid collision with other human machines.

Following above procedures and seeing mechanic regularly should keep your machine in tip-top running condition, far past warranty period. In fact, you may even become a smooth, polished "classic" someday.

CHAPTER IV
TREATMENT OF OTHERS

THE BEST WAY UP TO SUCCESS

FEW PERSONS are so vain or deluded anymore as to claim that they've climbed to success *all by themselves*, without the help of others. Many so-called self-made men used to claim they had, until it was pointed out to them that they had scrambled up over the bent backs of others. These days it is more common for a successful man to give much of the credit to others — "without whose loyal assistance I could never have reached the place where I am today."

We agree that no man gets to the top all by himself. One has helpers, willing or unwilling. If they're willing helpers, they're his friends, family, and associates. If they're unwilling helpers, they're his victims — the people he's used.

There are actually three ways in which you're helped to the top by others. One of these ways is bad, another one is okay, and the third is by far the best. They are: by stepping on others' feet; by standing on their shoulders; or by letting them stand on *your* shoulders. In other words, stepping on them is bad. Having them help you up is acceptable. But the best way is by helping *them* up.

What about that last one? How do you get to the top by lifting others up above yourself? Does that make sense?

You bet it does. Think about it a while. What's the most popular thing you can offer? Isn't it the thing that fulfills someone's needs? Well, then, if you fulfill someone's needs, aren't you helping him up?

That's the point. To learn someone's needs, you have to care about him. Fill his need and he'll start depending on you. And when folks depend on you, then you're up there. It's that simple.

MANNERS DO COUNT

WE WOULD do well to pay attention to our manners. In moments of hurry and worry, we may fail to practice our good manners. And manners, like music, must be practiced.

Some persons do not consider manners to be of much importance. Manners, they say, are just affectations. With such persons, we would argue this way: let them go through one day meeting only well-mannered clerks, receptionists, newsboys, drivers, and salesman, and then see how they feel at the end of that day. Then let them go through the next day encountering only rude and boorish ones, and see how they feel at the end of that day.

Good manners do make a lasting impression — not just on the person politely treated, but as well on the person who is being polite. Good manners usually hint at some deeper good. It has been said that "Good manners are the small coin of virtue," and that "Manners are minor morals." Or, as Horace Mann said, "Manners easily and rapidly mature into morals."

Each of us has the power, simply by practicing pleasant and respectful manners, to help smooth the path for everyone who comes along.

THE TOUGHEST OF ALL VIRTUES

PERHAPS the hardest of all virtues to sustain is that of unselfishness. Let no one say unselfishness is easy or comes naturally. Unselfishness is work of the toughest kind. And doubtless that is why so many people just won't do such work.

There are three main reasons why unselfishness is the hard work that it is.

First, it draws you away from your own desires. It uses up time you'd love to spend on yourself. It uses up energies you'd rather use for your own entertainment.

Second, the work of unselfishness grows and grows. When you do something unselfish, the word gets around that you're an unselfishness specialist — and then you are in demand. Everybody who ever heard of you thinks of something he'd like for you to do unselfishly for him. You become well-nigh indispensable. Every selfish so-and-so for miles around decides he needs you, because the selfish, of course, live as parasites on the unselfish.

Third, the work of unselfishness seems to pay you no regular wages and no time-and-a-half for overtime. Indeed, it seems *all* your time is overtime. You finish one job and instead of a paycheck someone brings you another job.

"Boy!" some smart cookie might say, "only some kind of a nut would get into that unselfishness racket! That'd break your back!"

And so it might. Maybe the unselfish person *is* some kind of a nut. But we have seen some really unselfish persons in our time, and if they were ever nuts, they were acorns from which strong and beautiful oaks have grown. It looked as if the burden had strengthened their backs instead of breaking them. Furthermore, it would appear that for every ounce of self they gave away, they received a pound of something greater. Call it contentment, call it stature, call it what you will; it is wealth greater than the selfish ever acquire. The unselfish end up with richness of spirit — and that wonderfully true thing called humility.

THE PUBLIC v. THE PRIVATE PERSON

MANY an admirable public figure, you may be sure, is something of a slob at home. Each of us is two persons — the public person and the private person. Behind the walls of home, a man is likely to be more true to his own nature than he is out in the world where so much is determined by protocol and appearances.

Probably it would be safe to say that in the majority of cases, the public man is a better behaved person than the private man — better mannered, more industrious, more thoughtful of his associates than he is of members of his family, whom he can take for granted.

And that is the pity of it. If indeed there must be a difference between the public man and the private man, it is a shame when the private man is worse than the public man. One should be his better self at home, not vice versa. The people who live within those walls with him are more important to him, and he is more important to them, than the ones he sees outside. He can bring his own family great happiness and good guidance; he can be a leader and a shaper of his home world, while his influence out in the world is negligible, even though he may think it is considerable.

Ideally, though, the public and the private person should be very much alike. Each should be as excellent as he can be, as considerate as he can be, as good an example as he can be. The satisfaction such a man could gain from being good with his family could add to the satisfaction he'd gain from being his best in public life.

For one should be at least as ambitious about earning the love and admiration of one's family as one is about gaining public honor and prestige.

HOW TO MAKE AN IMMORTAL SPLASH

JUST as each raindrop that falls on the ocean sends out small circular ripples, so every person's life in one way or another creates a temporary stir in the whole of mankind.

Some lives make bigger splashes than others, of course. Some make tidal waves. But even the most obscure is felt.

The momentary disturbance made by a life may be good or it may be bad. If one raindrop may nourish a flower, another may spoil a picnic.

Each of us is here for but a short time and, we must presume, for a reason. For one who does not believe his life signifies something, the moment of life must seem long and excruciating.

It is not always easy to see the importance of one's life, or to believe that one's presense on the scene makes a bit of difference. There are many millions of use on the earth at a time. Most of us never see our names in print (when they're printed in the birth announcements we're too young to read them, and when they're in the obituaries it's too late.) Few of us are ever asked for our autographs; the majority of us are not known outside our towns or neighborhoods. Few of us ever achieve anything that the rest of the world will remember us for. Sometimes we do, understandably, feel like raindrops falling unseen and unheeded, on a vast, gray sea, signifying nothing.

Perhaps this is the reason why people do try to acheive something. They want to count. They want to add something to the ocean of mankind. They want to make a splash, a wave, even a swell or a tide. As long as one believes that he can justify his moment of life, he does not despair or brood over his anonymity.

Nor is it the size of the splash that counts, so much as it is the goodness or badness of it. Witness the enormous and destructive evil surge set forth by a Hitler versus the briefest ripple of pleasure sent out by a person who generates smiles or a kind word.

Some feel that they will be more likely to make a noticeable splash by shocking, stunning, knocking down — by spoiling picnics. They may try to disturb the sea of anonymity around themselves by destroying property or perpetrating fraud or scandal. There are those who, if they cannot achieve fame legitimately, would do it through notoriety rather than go unnoticed.

How much better it would be, though, if they realized that it is more important to bring comfort to a few nearby friends than to bring bad headlines to a million readers.

Nothing is so underestimated as the consequences of a simple smile, a cheery word, a good deed. As the ripples from a drop go out and set other ripples in motion, a smile can cause another smile, and that another, ad infinitum. A good word creates the mood for another good word; a good deed is the example for a subsequent good deed.

One who originates a few of these each day, then, does more good than he may know. If he does this day in and day out, how can it be said that his life signifies nothing? And if he passes this goodness to his children, and they to theirs — there surely is immortality.

CHAPTER V
LOVE OF LIFE

BEING A "BARGAIN" FRIEND

LORD, help me to be a "bargain" friend. By that I mean, let those who come to me for friendship get more than they expected.

For what they give me in friendship, Lord, let me remember to try to give them still more.

Let them always go away from me surprised at the fullness of their hearts.

Let them always be pleased at the measure they have received from me. And remind me never to put my thumb on the scale when I am weighing out my love to them.

Let me always put an extra something, an unexpected pleasure, into the hours they spend with me.

Let me give them my best service and freest credit.

Let me keep my doors open to them at all hours.

Let my thoughts and words, which are my commodities, be always fresh and appealing.

May my friends never come to me for understanding and find it out of stock.

Let them never come to me for companionship and find it to be of poor quality.

May they never find my friendship to be more than they can afford, or even as much as they can afford.

Remind me never to deceive them with false advertisements of myself.

Thus, help me to be a "bargain" friend, O Lord, always.

And then if I find at last that I have given to them more than I've gotten in repayment, then I shouldn't at all mind going out of business that way.

37

LET'S NOT FORGET OUR SILENT PARTNERS

THE WIFE of the noted playwright George Bernard Shaw was fascinated by the character of St. Joan of Arc, and she thought Shaw could do an excellent play about her. However, Mrs. Shaw knew better than to tell her husband that he ought to write this or that; "the Genius," as she referred to him, was never receptive toward other peoples' suggestions. Instead, she began leaving books about Joan of Arc in conspicuous places all over the house. After some time of this, "the Genius" burst in excitedly one day and said, "Charlotte, I have a wonderful idea for a new play! It's about Saint Joan!" "Really?" she replied. "What a good idea!"

Shaw thereafter thought that the play, which was one of his best, was inspired by Saint Joan herself. And his wife was content to let him go on thinking that.

How many of us unwillingly owe a part of our success to one or more such silent partners? How many of us sit back smug about something we've done, never giving a bit of credit to the mates, friends, or associates who have helped, inspired, or encouraged us throughout the project? How many of us attribute our success to our own "genius" when actually there are many to whom we should be grateful?

We draw our ideas and our strength from many sources. Men have built empires based upon ideas given them by other men. Successful businessmen, statesmen, and artists have gotten where they are on rungs of moral support given by their families or friends. Examples like these are endless, but it is surely true to say that any successful or self-made man had at least one helping hand in his making. Let us never forget to give thanks for our benefactors — our often silent partners.

WHAT IS TOUGH LOVE?

WE ONCE heard someone use an unusual and very interesting phrase. "I decided," this person said, "that it was time for me to stop coddling and use some *tough love.*"

What is *tough love?* Well, it isn't the sort of thing you see in the private detective movies, where the "hero" softens the heroine up for a kiss by slapping her around. No, this kind of *tough love* is a real thing that ordinary people like us sometimes are forced to use on our dear ones — and sometimes they are forced to use on us.

Tough love is what you have to exert, for example, on someone who is wallowing in self-pity and won't come out of it to face up to the world. Finally, because of your love for that person and your desire to see him get back on his feet, you force yourself to talk straight to him. If he's using you as a crutch, you take his weight off yourself and make him stand on his own feet. Probably he will accuse you of being heartless and not caring for him. You have to be tough to listen to this, because inside you the full tenderness of your love is intact; and you have to be tough to stand your ground, because what you really want to do is continue giving comfort and sympathy.

This is but one example of what *tough love* is. Another commonplace example is the exercise of needed discipline on one's child. One spanks the child, thinking all the while, "This hurts me more than it does you."

Yes. It's a measure that sometimes must be taken. And *tough love* is a good way to describe it.

THE ART OF LOAFING

"BE INDUSTRIOUS." "Make hay while the sun shines." "Plough deep while sluggards sleep." These have been American slogans and proverbs for a long time now. In part because of them, we've become rich and progressive; we have accomplished fantastic things while less industrious peoples lagged. Simultaneously we've been taught that loafing is, if not a sin, a full-blown vice. Loafing has fallen into such disrepute that we feel guilty if we indulge in it.

It's unfortunate that we've lost the fine art of loafing. Our bodies and nerves suffer for the loss. If a man does not know how to loaf now and then, he can burn himself out, and wind up at forty-five years old a trembling, baggy-eyed knot of frayed nerves.

Work *is* good and noble and right. Achievement *is* the measure of the man; we won't argue with Benjamin Franklin and Elbert Hubbard about that. We will say, though, that loafing is a good and necessary thing, too — if it comes as a reward for good work and if the loafer loafs well.

Assuming that the reader agrees that loafing might be restorative and desirable, he might ask: How do I become a master of the art?

Well, most of the real masters, though their techniques differ, agree that the would-be loafer first should create the right surroundings, then attain the loafing state of mind.

The best environment for some may be indoors, but the true loafing greats advocate the outdoors. There must be no house chores, overdue correspondence, no neglected business reading within reach. Ideally, there should be no television or other artificial stimulants to numb the senses. The loafing place should be an island of non-involvement in the sea of business and cares.

Now the loafing state of mind consists simply of full receptiveness to every little thing in this island. If there is blue sky overhead, the loafer thinks of the beauty of blueness and thinks of what may be out in space beyond the blueness. If there is an oak tree nearby, the loafer considers the whole life cycle of that tree and the acorn from which it began. All his senses are open and his mind is freed from all encumbrances to flow backward into memory, outward into the present, upward to God, or onward to the future.

The loafer need not lie down or sit still to loaf effectively. He may walk, he may chew a grass stem, he may fish, he may play his harmonica or guitar. Best of all, he may play with his children or talk with them and heed what they say.

The loafing state of mind is a learning and healing state of mind. Tomorrow the loafer, strengthened and clear-eyed, will plunge back into the turbid sea of cares and business.

A GOOD PLACE TO VISIT

"IT'S HARD to find real fountain pen ink anymore," a friend told me. Things like flypaper, too, are rare. The last newsreel we saw in a theater, as we remember, was about the atom bomb and the surrender of Japan. Wax 78 rpm records have long since followed buggy whips down the road to oblivion.

Yet many people cling nostalgically to such things as the world charges on. They don't really like filling a drippy fountain pen or getting up and changing old phonograph records every few minutes, but they like to sigh and think, "Those were the days!" They cling to notions of bygone simplicities, bygone happiness, bygone opportunities, pleasures forever lost.

Such persons are not being fair to themselves. As one wit expressed it, "What enhances the good old days is a bad memory."

Still, it's a human habit to lament the passage of "better times" — which probably were not really better at all. We seek refuge in memories because that is easier and more comfortable than trying to swim upstream in the current of time.

The past is also popular because we cannot be called upon to do anything about it, as we are called upon to do something about the present and the future.

We would be better off to think of the past not as an Eden from which we've been driven, but as a library to which we can refer back for the knowledge and wisdom we need as we chart the future.

"The past was a nice place to visit," said our friend, "but I wouldn't want to live there."

START A GOOD WORD RELAY RACE TODAY

WE'VE all seen how a relay race is run. At the starting gun, one runner starts off, carrying the baton. After he's carried the baton a certain distance, he passes it on to a new runner who has taken up his stride; then another runner takes the baton and runs with it. The starting runner and second runner do not participate in the final crossing of the finish line. But the baton does, and then the whole winning relay team shares the triumph.

In a similiar way, you can start a relay race at any time of the day simply by speaking a good, kind word to somebody. The good word represents the baton; the person you say it to will carry it for a short while, then bestow it upon another carrier. This race can go on all day, with that good word being carried untiringly by one teammate after another. Everybody in the team shares in the triumph of it. In fact, there isn't even a loser in this kind of a relay race. You can pass the baton and yet keep it — and keep on running with it. You can send it off in one direction and two seconds later send it off carried by someone else in another direction, and still have it yourself.

There are capable people who keep up these good-word relays nearly every day of their lives. Sometimes one of these will make you a runner in one of his relays before you know what's happening: suddenly, out of a clear blue sky, he's given you the baton, a cheering word, and your impulse is to carry it for your leg of the race and pass it along. Soon you realize how great it feels to be relaying good will along.

Chances are you'll get to the point where you like it so well that, if nobody comes along and passes you a baton, you start one of your own.

LOVE HAS THE ANSWERS

"Man lernt nichts kennen als was man liebt."
Johann Wolfgang vonGoethe

WHAT a truth the great German poet uttered when he said: "Man learns to understand only what he loves." Everything that man does not love mystifies and sometimes frightens him. But if he learns to love it, then his understanding of it follows more easily. Does this sound like an oversimplification, as maxims sometimes do? Well, if it does, let us test it by applying it to things we know — basic, important things like one's mate, one's work, and one's life.

Could a man ever learn to understand his wife's actions or words or feelings if he did not truly love her? Not likely, because if he were not deeply in love with her he could not give enough attention to those actions or words or feelings. It takes a lot of a man's concentration to make him learn that when she says, "We can't go; I haven't a thing to wear," she really means, "Tell me what you like me best in." And so on.

Could a man ever learn to understand all the aspects of his job if he did not love work? Not likely, because if he did not love it, he would never be motivated to study it and apply himself to it. Granted, he might learn enough by rote to perform the necessary functions of the job, but he would be frustrated and suspicious of its whys and hows.

Could a man ever learn to make heads or tails of this bizarre, baffling struggle called life, if he did not love life? Indeed not! Because he could not recognize a joy or a triumph even if it fell in his lap. It would be all futility and despair; the very fact of his having been born would seem an imposition. *Man lernt nichts kennen als was man liebt.*

CHAPTER VI
SPIRIT AND GRATITUDE

SNAPBACK

IT'S A RARE plan that doesn't go awry, a rare scheme that doesn't fall through sooner or later, a rare enterprise that doesn't suffer a fatal mistake, a rare dream that isn't one day blown apart by a blast of bad fortune. We might as well face that hard fact as we build our castles in air or throw ourselves into great loves and projects. Sooner or later it's all likely to come tumbling down. We all know that from experience.

But it doesn't matter how many times you're knocked down, just as long as you get back to your feet one more time. To get back up after a downfall requires a certain tough exuberance. Getting up sadly and sobbingly is the hardest way. Trying to find respite in the bottom of a highball glass is morbid and unnatural. To blame anyone else, including Dame Fortune, and lie there groaning about the unfairness of it, eats up the soul.

No. What's required is a quick and exuberant rebound — snapback. No time squandered on self-pity or blame. No escaping into remorse. Only you can crush your own spirit. Failure cannot crush it. Failure is outside you, where it can't crush you, unless you let it come in and fall heavily on your spirit.

If your present dream collapses, pause a moment. Lean back in your chair. Look out a window at the sky. Hold the hand of a loved one and absorb its warmth. Feel relieved that that old venture is past. Whistle. Smile at the indestructibility of your soul and then put your brain to work on the next dream. Hope is like stoneware, not like a paper plate. It can be used over and over again, and it will never wear out.

THAT MAGIC WORD

PLEASURE! What a magical word! Man's dream of heaven is an eternity of uninterrupted pleasure. But by wishing for this, man reveals his ignorance of himself. He ought to know from experience that pleasure is pleasure only when and because it is brief and occasional. Robert Burns wrote, ". . . pleasures are like poppies spread: You seize the flow'r, its bloom is shed; Or like the snow falls in the river, a moment white — then melts forever . . . Or like the rainbow's lovely form Evanishing amid the storm."

Let us thank God that pleasures are forever fleeting and teasing, forever anticipated and remembered, but only for an instant held. Because it is man's nature that he is always distracted, easily bored, and if pleasure lasted for hours or days, he would become impatient with it; he would think it monotonous and thereby he would destroy forever its value as a pleasure. Then, soon, he would have used all his pleasures up.

After that, what sort of heaven could he dream of all the time?

AIM-THROUGH AND FOLLOW-THROUGH

THERE'S an old saying that if you want to surmount something that seems almost impossible, the thing to do is "throw your heart over; the rest will follow."

Someone asked a karate expert how it was possible for him to drive his hand through a board. His reply was: "You don't aim at the board, you aim through it." In other words, you don't think of the hard surface of the board as your target, you think of the other side of it as the place where your hand is going to go. So, when your hand hits that surface, the blow isn't over, it's still going on. That way, the board doesn't stop it.

Or consider the remarks of the golfer famous for his long, powerful drives. If he aims only at the ball, he says, the power of his stroke tends to end at the ball. Instead, he thinks of that white ball as merely a point through which the club has to pass as the swing is being made. How many golfing experts have repeatedly said that the follow-through is the important part of the shot?

This seems to be the way it is in life as well. You don't want to aim at your life's goal, you want to aim through it. Think of somebody you know whose goal, for example, was retirement. What happened when he reached retirement? Chances are, his life just sort of fell apart. He was past the target point and found that he was just plain done. In other words, he didn't have any follow-through still carrying him along.

A research psychologist for the Veteran's Administration once made a study which indicated that people live for as long as they feel needed and useful. "If the older individual has a need for the years beyond 70, he will retain competence and live longer," said the psychologist. He indicated that if a person keeps working until the age of 100, he may live to be 120 or even 140 years old.

And that's not just theory. In several areas of the world there are societies in which unusual numbers of the elderly continue to do useful work and live far past the century mark, many remaining active to 120 years of age or more. Scientists have deduced that it is the following combination of factors that account for their robust old age: continuing usefulness, physical activity, active participation in the family, and a generally low caloric intake. Evidently, say the scientists, these lively old men and women have no notion that they'll be "used up" by age 65 or 70, so they just keep on living and enjoying it.

In other words, they have strong follow-through. The evidence is that a good life with intentional follow-through can contribute a great deal to longevity. Much more than we've been led to believe.

47

MUSINGS ON COURAGE

IT IS our courage that makes us worthwhile. It is courage that makes us stand our ground and see things through. It is courage that drives us onward in the face of difficulty so that we may improve the world and ourselves. It has been man's courage in its many forms that has made him the noble and inspired creature that he is.

Courage means heart. *Cor. Coeur. Corage. Courage* — the word comes from old words meaning "heart." In poems and songs, the strong-hearted one is the hero. It was the strong-hearted one who faced a giant and slew him with a slingshot. It was the strong-hearted one who sailed into unknown waters. It was the strong-hearted One who carried His own cross up to the place of His execution.

But courage is not the exclusive property of soldiers and saints, explorers and martyrs, of heroes of antiquity. Courage is of the here and now, of every man and woman. No matter how tame and humdrum the modern workaday world may seem, no matter how mild and regimented the people may seem, courage is still courage and as essential as ever. Courage is still the strength of heart that will not let us back down from what we dread.

Today, instead of lions and giants threatening to kill our bodies, we fight those vague influences that threaten to kill our spirit. We fight boredom and faithlessness. Instead of sailing Columbus' uncharted seas, toward what was feared to be the edge of the world, we navigate the Nuclear Age, which is feared to be the end of the world. Today, instead of a wooden cross, we stagger under a measureless weight of doubts and debts. Today, instead of the one-eyed Cyclops or the mysterious spells of island witches, we face the monster of our own technology and the depressing puzzle of a sick environment.

Our time, we fear, seems to be running out. How are we to stay stout-hearted in the face of extinction, ennui, and a future with no marked ideological pathways?

Well, any hero of the past also thought his time was running out. He thought he was doomed and lost, too. We are not the first to be so afraid. But the heroes of the past summoned up all the strength that their hearts could pump out, all the faith their souls could draw down from an unseen god, and waded into what they feared. And that is what we will do.

Courage, say wise men, does not mean the absence of fear; it means walking forward into what we fear.

Courage is the test by which we determine whether we are worthy to be called human.

Suppose that no man had ever the courage to oppose the tyranny of the tribal strong man. Suppose that no man had ever had the courage to go beyond a familiar horizon. Suppose that no man had ever risked being ridiculed by his fellows to present a new idea. Suppose no man had ever had the courage to make his heart vulnerable by loving. Where would we be now? Strictly nowhere.

TAKE INVENTORY OF YOUR BLESSINGS

WE'VE all got well-being that we aren't even aware of — but we certainly can't say that about our miseries. Most of us publicize a daily report of our miseries. But we seldom remark on our blessings. Not to others, and usually we don't even acknowledge them to ourselves.

Why don't we get into the habit of taking inventories of our blessings regularly?

Take a look at yourself. What have you got? We don't mean property or belongings. Those as often as not are problems. But look at yourself.

Have you got two fairly good feet and legs? If you don't think those are blessings, try getting around with one or none of them.

Have you got two good hands that open and close? If you think those aren't blessings, try getting dressed or fixing breakfast with one of them tied behind your back.

Have you got a few good teeth in your head? Even if you only have two — well juxtaposed — you're comparatively well off. And how about those eyes and ears and nostrils and taste buds that open you out onto the marvels and beauties of the world around you? Do you ever thank your Maker for those? Not many of us do very often.

And then, above all, how about that infinite expanse of spirit

49

that is truly you? It is your you-ness, and it can appreciate every experience from the slightest tickle or caress up to the immense rapture of accepting your God. That spirit of yours is without limits, outward or inward, if you wish it to be. Through the inward regard of your spirit, you may look deeper and deeper to the soul's depth; through the outward vision of spirit, you may look deeper and deeper beyond the stars, until the two looks meet and you realize that both mysteries are one and the same.

But you have to let your spirit experience greatly, and that means you have to appreciate and value your spirit and nourish it — just as you have to appreciate your limbs and your senses and use them to their best advantage.

Most people's lives are disgustingly, depressingly small. Their miseries are overvalued and considered too much; their blessings are all but ignored.

Within your unprepossessing hide, you're a treasure house of God-given blessings. But you'll never know it unless you take an inventory.

UNDER THE SURFACE

WE JUST happened to be walking alongside a stream the other day, a stream which flows southwestward. As streams do, it always flows in the same direction.

But this particular day there was a brisk spring wind blowing from the southwest, making choppy waves and chasing them upstream, and if we had not been so well acquainted with that stream, we would have thought from the looks of it that that water was going toward the northeast.

Seeing that phenomenon made us think a bit on a few things:

How much like that stream is the relationship between history and current events. We follow the news of the world daily, and we seem to see everything frantically dashing and splashing along one way. But a quarter of a century from now we will see that the news — that is, the surface of events — was appearing to go one way, while underneath it the deep currents of history were going the other way.

Or how much like that stream are our acquaintances. For one reason or another — to make a sale, or to butter us up, they may indicate in their expressions or actions a great accord with us, while, underneath, they don't care for us much at all. On the other hand, our true friends, who have a strong and deep under-current of love for us, may flare up at us, frown at us and criticize us — probably because we're temporarily disappointing them in some way. There again, we see the visible waves on the surface going one way while the invisible and more important current is going the other way.

And how much like that stream our troubles can be: frothy waves wetting and chilling us, while underneath, our lives flow irresistibly toward betterment.

How foolish we'd be, to judge things only by their surfaces!

SOMETHING SPECIAL

WHAT IS it that there is so much of, free for the taking, and yet so few persons seem to have? It takes you farther than a car, and doesn't cost one five-thousandth as much. Yet almost everybody has a car and almost nobody seems to have this thing we're talking about. It's more fascinating than a color television and seldom needs repair, yet more people seem to have color TVs than have this thing. You can live more comfortably in this thing than in a suburban ranch home, and you don't have to pay a property tax on it, yet more persons seem to live in ranch homes than in this thing we're talking about. This thing can purchase more good living for you than a ton of money. Yet you don't have to guard it or worry about inflation eating away its buying power. What is this mysterious thing that is so great to have and anyone can have free and yet so few persons seem to seek?

ANSWER: Faith.

CHAPTER VII
TEACHING, LEARNING, AND THINKING

THESE THINGS ARE ALWAYS TRUE

BETWEEN the times when we were born and our children were born, many new things and ideas came into being. So many, in fact, that our children are growing up in a world that is not very much like the world in which *we* grew up. And, at the rate things are still changing, our children's children will be growing up in a world quite different from the present one.

What, then, does this rapid metamorphosis mean to the parents who have the responsibility for preparing their sons and daughters for the living of life? It means that lessons may cease to be valid even while they are being taught. It is like the remark of the speeding motorist: "Up ahead is a very small town we're passing through, wasn't it?" That is to say, by the time we've put the world as we see it into words, it's too late for the words to mean anything. And the young, listening to those lessons, look around them and say, "But it really isn't like that." And you, their teacher, look up, astonished, and exclaim: "You're right, it isn't. But it *was*, the last time I looked!"

What, then, should we as parents do? Give up trying to teach? Let our children simply plunge into the mainstream of life to sink or swim? No. Because there are some lessons concerning life that hold true always, whatever life may be like at any given moment.

If the things we have been teaching our children are not valid anymore, it is because we have been teaching them the things that are true only under certain circumstances — things that were once true, temporarily true, things that were true under the system that prevailed in our day — rather than the things that remain always true.

And these things that are always true are really the best preparation for life; they are like basic swimming lessons which prepare a swimmer to swim in any waters.

These changing, temporary truths have to do with such matters as who has authority, what should our goals be, what are the trappings of status, what is ethical, what is tolerable, what is seemly, what is stylish, what is funny, what is acceptable. On these ever-changing matters, generations can hardly be expected to agree. Yet these are the things we try so hard to teach, as if we expected them always to be just what they were in our own time.

But those things that hold true always, what are they? Well, they are things like the Golden Rule. The importance of self-sacrifice and self-reliance. The joy of being warm-hearted and big-minded. The nobility of the worker who is conscientious about his work. The appreciation of our natural earth and the mankind upon it. The importance of original thinking. Faith in the gradual betterment of the human race. The necessity of tolerance and peace. The beauty of gentleness and good humor.

These are some of the constant things, the eternally important things. These, unfortunately, are also the things that too many of us gloss over while teaching our young, and that our elders glossed over while teaching us.

Perhaps too much time is devoted to teaching the temporary formulas for making a living — while too little is devoted to the eternal formulas for making a life.

THE LIBRARY OF YOUR MIND

THINK of your mind as a library. A very personal library, full of the tragedies, comedies, manuals, glossaries, and the drab daily journals of your life. Everything that has happened to you is recorded in there; everything you have studied is stored there; all your dreams and plans and secrets are tucked away in dark and dusty recesses or on the front shelves.

There, too, are some volumes of the deepest significance, and there are thousands of loose-leaf sheets scrawled over with un-classified, unfiled trivia. In every mind's library, there are holy books as well as profane and obscene ones. It does not matter who you are, your mind holds much that is worthy and much that is unworthy.

The important thing about your mind — that thing upon which you would be judged — is not what the library of your mind contains, but what you use of it — what you refer to and ponder on. What you take out and thumb through thoughtfully, that which you study and live by — that's what is important.

If you keep shuffling through the scribbled scraps or peeking into the dirty books, or mumbling over hateful slogans, or browsing dumbly through the dreary pages of your own petty diaries, while the great and exciting lessons lie ignored and moulding, that is certainly not to your credit. You're misusing that precious library. But if you refer frequently to the proverbs or the great and ennobling ideas therein, your days will be enriched.

GET A MENTAL CHARLEY HORSE

YOU KNOW how it is when, after a long winter without any physical exercise to speak of, you go out one spring day and play catch or touch football or tennis with your son. By evening, strange sensations are settling into your joints and sinews, and you're looking forward to bedtime. The next morning is agony. You feel as if your leg bones and arm bones had grown twice as long and your muscles had shortened by half. It feels as if every tendon were done up in a granny knot.

The thing that's hard to realize on that painful morning is that this pain represents something good. It means that your muscles are getting toned up. You doubt that you can get down to tie your shoelaces, but the fact is that you've become a little more fit.

Well, it's the same way with hard, active thinking. If you've gotten into the habit of slouching mentally, if you've had a long spell of adopting other people's opinions and generalizing on

55

your own, well, the first time you really hammer out a thought of your own you're liable to get a mental charley horse from the effort.

Carrying a thought from its conception to its conclusion is as strenuous as twisting and speeding down the field to the goal line. In the game, you dodge your opponent, who can stop you short of the goal if he gets his hands on you. In your thinking, you try to dodge all your prejudices and your preconceived notions which will do their best to stop you somewhere short of reaching a real conclusion.

In other words, real, hard thinking is no sissy game. You can end up with a headache. All your old, flabby ideas will lie about bruised and strained because they've been hit so hard and stretched so far. But the pain means you're more mentally fit than you were before.

YOUR COMPANION FOR LIFE

YOU HAVE a constant companion. It is with you all your life. It can either be your greatest comfort or your most terrible torment — or both. This companion is your own mind.

Your mind may be a source of great wisdom and counsel, or a petty chatterbox of trivia and troubles. Your mind may be your final arbiter in all important decisions or, on the other hand, a confuser of the simplest issues, making the easiest choice impossible.

Your mind may be for you an artist, a poet, and an entertainer, providing you with lovely pictures, delightful notions, and ready humor. On the other hand, your mind may be a dark and cheerless curtain which blanks out the beauty of everything and muffles the music of laughter.

Your mind might be your important partner in hopeful endeavors giving you original ideas and exciting approaches; on the other hand, it might be your fiercest rival, belittling your ambitions and undercutting your every effort.

Your mind might be the white steed that carries you lightly

over the rocks and deserts of trouble and loneliness, or it might be a dark and heavy parasite that rides on your shoulders and makes your feet sink even deeper into the bogs of despair which we all, at times, must wade.

Your mind may bear a torch of the light of understanding before you all through your life, or it may lay down gloomy smoke-screens and strew rubble in your path as you try to grope toward the meaning of life.

This is your constant companion, this mind. If it is alert and cheerful, you are in the best of company. If not — then pity for you.

THIS IS SELECTIVITY

THE MAN who claims that reading bores him is probably the man who waits until he has nothing else to do, then strolls into the drugstore and desultorily picks from the book racks some book with a particularly lurid cover.

The man who claims that there's nothing interesting on radio or television is probably the man who switches them on the moment he gets into the house and leaves them on until bedtime or past, half-listening until he's stupefied by the constant noise.

The man who complains that people are dumb and dull is probably the man who spends all day idling his hours away with small talk, old off-color jokes, gossip, and back-biting.

The man who complains that life is a drag, no fun, who says nothing interesting ever happens, is likely the man who expects to be amused all day and is surprised that other people in the world have more important things to do besides providing amusement for him.

On the other hand, the man who finds great pleasure in reading and wisdom in books is the man who discriminately seeks meaningful literature beforehand, then anticipates the moment when he'll have the opportunity to sit down and read it with full attention. The one who finds something worthwhile on radio or television is the one who turns it on only when there is something scheduled that he is truly eager to see or hear. The one who loves people and finds them fascinating is the one who is sincerely interested in the deeper part of their thoughts — their philosophies of life.

And the man who enjoys life is the man who, in the middle of the day's drudgery, can catch and appreciate those golden moments and gemlike words that only a discriminating spirit can perceive.

What we are saying is that unless one is selective about what he takes in through his senses, his whole soul can become glutted — and, like a stuffed diner, he finds no savor in anything.

The world around us is an infinitude of things; we are flooded over with impressions and novelities and distractions. Yet we have so little time to waste on the vast array of meaningless things. One of the important responsibilities of a man's intelligence is to detect what is meaningful, winnow out the chaff from the good, and to grasp and cherish only what is uplifting in life.

This is selectivity. The happiest persons are those who have learned to seek and find the grains of spiritual gold in the measureless mess of worldly chaff.

THE SECRET OF GREAT TEACHERS

HISTORIANS tell us that many teachers of the young in ancient times were such spellbinders that they could convene their pupils on wooded hillsides or in flowery glades and keep them so enthralled with learning that they did not drift off in search of play.

This they accomplished without a single million-dollar school building, without audio-visual teaching aids, without school psychologists or swimming pools. These great teachers managed to hold their pupils' attention and made them want to learn more than they wanted anything else. How did they do it, we wonder? With magic?

Yes, the answer is just that. Magic.

Magic has always been the most important ingredient in teaching. It was when we were children and it still is.

Let us think back. Whether we studied in one-room country schools or in the dim and steamy classrooms of big city schools, most of us were fortunate enough to have at least one teacher who resorted to this ancient magic. It might have been a gray-haired spinster in a dark dress, or a lean, balding man with some indefinable spark behind his wire-rimmed spectacles. The thing we remember is that, when he or she called the class to order and pulled shut the classroom door, the blackboards and pencil scarred desks faded away and we were being transported along the enchanted corridors of thought and the mystical realms of knowledge. The names of old heroes and extinct civilizations rang in our ears; we imagined trumpet calls and the tread of sandaled feet.

As taught by such teachers, scientific and mathematical terms refreshed us with their neat precision. In our imaginations, we lurked among arteries and lymph nodes, raced along primary nerves, and caught tantalizing glimpses of the secret of life. We swam in the deep waters of the river of history and stared eagerly ahead into the stellar distances of the future. We turned songs and poems over in our brains as we would hard candies on our tongues. And when the class bell rang, it was as if we had come back to earth from some other worldly region where colors were brighter and sounds more musical. It was simply that we had been under the spell of magic — that particular priceless kind called teacher's magic.

We would like to be able to define that magic, but it is just too complex, too personal, too delicate for analysis. But there is one thing in it that we can be sure of: the teacher who has this magical power is the teacher who rejoices in the miracle of life and wants others to share the same joy.

This is the teacher who hopes people will grow up still looking at the world through the eager and wondering eyes of children.

This is the teacher who finds nature and mankind richly curious, and cherishes the chance to infect others' minds with curiosity.

So there — though perhaps oversimplified — is the stuff of great teachers: *magic*, the kind that brings time and space and wonderment into a classroom.

59

CHAPTER VIII
CHARACTER

BEING ONE'S OWN MAN

ONE OF the best things that can be said about a man is that "he is his own man." As they used to say, "When they made him, they threw the mold away." This is the man who builds his own character naturally, instead of looking around for someone else's characteristics to copy. This is the man who is too big and too busy to waste time imitating the trappings and manners of his neighbor. This is the man who cannot be coerced into speaking others' opinions instead of his own.

Imitators don't quite know what to make of such a man. They may detest and fear him for staying outside their pattern; on the other hand, they may start imitating him. It doesn't bother him, either way. He does not ask them to approve of his manner or to be like him. He is not consciously trying to be different from them, he is only being himself. He is too occupied with living life to be concerned about leading or following fashions. He worries not about seeming different, undifferent, or indifferent; such worries take time from more important concerns.

Not every man who is his own man will be known as a great man. But no man who is not his own man will be known as a great man.

SUPERPERSON

MANY YEARS ago, we and most of our fellow youngsters used to pore over the Superman comic books and entertain fantastic daydreams of how great it would be to be as strong, swift, and invincible as that dauntless character.

The trouble is, we just dreamed about it and then grew up never doing anything about it, even though we could have.

Not that we could have become bullet-proof, fire-resistant, shrink-proof, and wrinkle-resistant as that great caped hero was. Of course not. But any mortal can make an inspired and continual effort to become a Superperson, if only he will.

Most of us are lucky enough to be able to count at least one Superperson among our friends, relatives, or acquaintances, so we know Superpersons do exist. Probably the Superpersons we know do not have muscles of steel, broad chests, or X-ray vision, nor are they indestructible; those are only a cartoonist's simplistic and symbolic interpretations of Superness. No, indeed. The real, honest-to-goodness kind of Superperson may have a weak chin, varicose veins, and a milder manner than Clark Kent's.

The Superness in a Superperson is inside him (or her) and was developed there conscientiously through the years. That Superness is more commonly known as character. It is composed of integrity, compassion, courage, humor, selflessness, and forbearance, mixed in varying proportions. Only the backbone is steely. Only the spirit is indestructible. The only walls the vision can penetrate are the walls of other peoples' hearts. Superpersons are spiritually Super, not physically. Anybody can become a Superperson. Why don't more of us try?

MY BOSS IS A TYRANT

MY BOSS is a tyrant. My boss is a slave driver. My boss insists that I be punctual and do a bang-up job every minute of the day. If I am late or sloppy in my work, I really catch it from my boss. And when my boss chews me out, I really have to listen because he knows all about me, and he can hit my faults right on the button.

My boss is always looking right over my shoulder, and if I make a mistake, he's right there where he can give me a hard kick where it hurts most. But even worse, he follows me everywhere I go, even after working hours, and nags me about my mistakes.

Even when I manage to do something right, he thinks I could have tried just a little harder and done it a little better. It doesn't do me any good to argue that I did the best I could under the circumstances. He retorts that he knows the circumstances better that I do and won't accept them as excuses.

Yes. My boss is a real tyrant. But, you know, I'm really glad he is: because my boss is my own integrity.

A DIFFERENT VIEW

WHY IS IT, whenever I get in a group of people, that some boring fool would rather talk to me about his own dull self than listen to me talk about my own fascinating self? Why would he rather tell his own corny jokes than listen to my hilarious ones? What in the world is it that makes him think his appendectomy or bursitis is anywhere near as interesting as mine? Where does he get the idea that his children's sayings are as clever as mine's? Where does he ever get the crazy notion that his religious and political convictions are more valid than mine? Who does he think is the center of the universe, anyway, him or me?

FAILERS AND SUCCEEDERS

WHAT'S the main difference between the success and the failure? We would venture that the successful person is the one who forces himself to do all the necessary but unpleasant things that the failer avoids.

You've probably noticed that every kind of job, no matter how much you basically like it, has aspects that are pure drudgery or are in some way downright unpleasant. Maybe it requires more attention to detail than you like to give. Maybe it requires that you start earlier, move faster, or push harder than you like. Maybe it requires that you pay more attention to others instead of indulging yourself. Maybe it puts you on the firing line when you'd rather fade into the background.

Every job has some of these rough aspects. And we'd guess that the man who ultimately succeeds is the one who pockets his selfish desires, sets his teeth, then puts his hands and mind to the whole task — the fun part and the miserable part alike. And the man who fails? Well, we've all seen him in action. He shuns, postpones, or just plain turns his back on, the tasks that he dislikes, trying to drift along through the pleasant duties.

The failer, we might say, is short-sighted. He thinks he can be happier day by day avoiding the rough spots. The succeeder has longer vision. He knows that if he meets all his responsibilities day by day, he's going to learn more, help more people, earn more esteem, and — end up with a clear conscience and full self-respect.

OUT OF THINE OWN MOUTH...

THE TEMPTATION is strong to attack an enemy by saying bad things about him. Whether he is your rival in business, someone who has fired you from your job, someone who has gotten the best of you in a deal, or whatever, you tend to malign him, either by outright slander or by innuendo. You want to wage a propaganda war against that person whenever you can and make everybody else dislike him as much as you do. Perhaps you do this to gain sympathy for yourself as much as to cause him harm.

But whatever your motive or your methods, take this advice: don't do it. It isn't worth it. It doesn't work out the way you expect. It's self-defeating.

People may believe you, of course. They may agree with you that, yes, that sure must be one awful person. But at the same time they're likely to be saying to themselves, "Well, I certainly wouldn't want this guy saying things like that about me." They might look at you and nod, saying that they see your point, but ironically they may be feeling just a bit of sympathy for the other person because of the way you're talking about him. At any rate, they are quite likely to think less of you for having such a loose and vicious mouth.

Besides that, you damage your own self-esteem by pouring out such vitriol. It's even more important what you think of yourself than what others think of you. If you suddenly realize how petty and nasty you've been, you lose even your righteousness. Then you're truly the loser.

TOO BIG

THERE was an expression parents used to use to squelch kids who seemed to be thinking too greatly of themselves: "Don't get too big for your britches!" Remember?

Nowadays, that warning might serve better as a slogan for dieters. But is still has its validity insofar as keeping people properly humble is concerned. Humility is one of the sweetest virtues. To be humble (don't get us wrong) doesn't mean to belittle yourself, it simply means to keep yourself in the right perspective. A proper measure of humility makes the difference between a "big man" and a great man—the great one being the one with the humility. Clergyman Caleb Colton once said: "Subtract from the great man all that he owes to opportunity, all that he owes to chance, and all that he has gained by the wisdom of his friends and the folly of his enemies, and the giant will often be seen to be a pigmy."

So, succeed and grow all you can. But don't get too big for your britches.

LEADERSHIP

IT HAS been said that if twenty men, identical in age and education, were set down in completely new surroundings with equal opportunities, one of them would surely be leader of the group within a week. Men just naturally find their own innate levels as leaders or followers.

But what are the qualities that put a man in a position of leadership? What is it about him that makes others willing to entrust their fortunes and destinies to him? Why will thousands of persons look for guidance to one man when important things — even their lives — may be at stake?

One could fill pages with words describing the traits of a leader. Thinking of George Washington, one could say a leader has dignity and courage. Thinking of Abraham Lincoln, one could say a leader has humanism and faith. Thinking of Winston Churchill, one could say a leader has eloquence and wisdom. And, thinking of Christ, one could say that a leader has love for mankind.

A leader may have any or all of those qualities, in various degrees. But if his leadership is to endure, he probably will need, above all, an unshakable belief in people. Cynical men, with little respect for human lives, do not lead well or for long. Walt Whitman once said he was troubled by seeing "large masses of men following the lead of those who do not believe in men."

"Fail to honor people, they fail to honor you," wrote Lao-Tse. Then he added: ". . . . of a good leader . . . . when his work is done, his aim fulfilled, the people will say, 'We did this ourselves.'"

TRY FLEXING YOUR WILL

IT IS EASY to stop short of doing some unpleasant thing, and then excuse oneself by thinking something like: "Well, by nature I am shy and not aggressive. By nature I live and let live." Very often we make such excuses for what really is merely laziness of the will.

Oh, yes, there is such a thing as laziness of the will, just as there is laziness of the muscles. Think of the two for a moment and compare them. If you are going to push a desk across the room you first put your hand against the desk's weight. Then, for an instant, the working muscle will tense or flex before the desk begins to move.

In this sense, will power is just like muscle power. Remember what it was like the last time you had to say something that was not easy or be strong when it would have been easier to be weak? Remember how you took a breath and "flexed" your will for

66

the task? You could almost feel it. And then you could feel it starting to move the "weight."

Like muscle power, will power in action is not at all unpleasant. Once it gets the weight going, it enjoys the motion it has caused; it is not nearly so bad as the lazy sense of dread you felt before starting.

And the similarity goes one step farther: at night, after your muscles have pushed and lifted in honest labor through the day, they feel a good, warm weariness — not the restless lethargy they would have felt if you had lazed all day. So it is with the will. It is a good feeling at the end of the day, not to have to make excuses for the laziness of the will.

CHAPTER IX
BELIEFS

A CHANGE OF DREAMS

JUST A FEW years ago, a certain man used to dream a very typical dream of retirement. He envisioned himself living out quiet, lazy, and sunshiny days on a pastoral farm, surrounded by whispering trees, plenty of books and grandchildren, and flower gardens, with unhurried hours to enjoy leisure and beauty.

For many years, while working long hours in the strain of business, he nurtured that idyllic dream; he could take refuge in the very thought of it, refuge from the ugliness, hurry, and personal commitment of his business world.

As he grew older, his work began to demand more and more of him. His duties veered toward the older and uglier parts of the city. He began counseling failing little firms and shops down in the dingy sections of the inner city. He worked with people who were desperate and ready to give up, teaching them how to earn more on their investments, how to keep better books, how to inject some vigor into their run down shops and factories, how to keep their employees happy, how to reverse the disintegration of their neighborhoods.

Before long, he found himself spending his own time in the evenings counseling individuals on their personal problems. These poor people found him a source of strength and good advice, not only in business matters but also in their personal troubles. He was a sympathetic listener and also a resourceful doer.

But as he became more and more embroiled in the struggles of these people, he had less and less time for his daydream. His dream farm, his place of beauty, seemed to be drifting farther out of his grasp.

69

Gradually, in places where the storefronts had been shabby and peeling, where vacant lots had been full of rusty cans and broken bottles, where sidewalks had been crumbling and littered, where gloom had peeked out of broken windows, where children had fought with sticks and rocks and had damaged property in their boredom, the effects of his work began to show up. Property began to be repaired. Employment picked up. People began to help and trust each other. Fewer kids dropped out of school. Flowers appeared in window boxes. In the streets one could hear fewer curses and more laughter.

And this man, now almost physically exhausted, finally had his chance to retire to his dream farm. He thought about it. But his dream had changed a bit. And so, when he sold his house in the suburbs, he did not buy a farm in the country. Instead, he took an apartment right in the heart of the inner city. There was still so much work to be done, and he wanted to be right there where he could work on it.

He explains now, as he sits in his apartment looking out on the gray rooftops: "Somehow, my idea of beauty has changed. Oh, I still love nature and peace. But now I see the deepest kind of beauty in the faces and the actions of people. I see it in the smiles of folks who have overcome troubles. Beauty is not just in sunsets and leafy glades; it is, above all, in what people do."

"True beauty," he continued smiling thoughtfully, "is in people. And here it shines like a pearl right in the heart of ugliness, lovely in its contrast. I'm very content with my new dream."

THE PERFECT RULE TO GO BY

SUPPOSE a man has a difficult choice to make. For many reasons, he knows he will benefit from one course of action. For other reasons, he knows that another course of action would make life easier on somebody else. So the agonizing question for him is, "Which should I do?" Every one of us has to wrestle with such a choice now and then. Sometimes, among all the rules of ethics we've been taught, there doesn't seem to be one strong enough or fair enough to swing the decision for us.

But there *is* one rule that applies to every such dilemma. It is a rule that has been distilled out of all the advice and counsel of all the wise men of all the great civilizations.

Centuries ago, Confucius, the great practical wise man of China, wrote: "What you would not wish done to yourself, do not do unto others."

Gautama Buddha taught that, "One should seek for others the happiness one desires for oneself."

The Hindu Scriptures say, "The true role of life is to guard and do by the things of others as one would by his own."

In the Egyptian *Book of the Dead*, it is inscribed: "He sought for others the good he desired for himself; let him pass on."

In ancient Greece, it was advised: "Do not that to a neighbor which you would take ill from him," and in Persia it was, "Do as you would be done by."

"The law imprinted on the hearts of all men," said Roman sages, "is to love the members of society as themselves."

And Mohammed wrote: "Let none of you treat his brother but in a way you yourself would like to be treated."

"Do as you would be done by, is the surest method of pleasing," wrote the Earl of Chesterfield in the 18th century.

In Judaism, the Talmud says: "What is hateful to you, do not to your fellowmen. That is the entire law; all the rest is commentary."

It comes up in the writings of every major religion and every advanced civilization. It is paraphrased in each, but it is always recognizable. It is the Golden Rule, and we know it best in Christ's words: "All things whatsoever ye would that men should do to you, do ye even so to them."

Well, then. Wonder of wonders! Here is a statement so simple and wise and obvious that it has been considered the final answer in all ages; it is probably the only thing that all the wise men and prophets throughout history ever agreed on. There really must be something to it. Martin Luther said of The Golden Rule that if it were carried out, "then everything would instruct and arrange itself; then no law books nor courts nor judicial actions would be required; all things would quietly and simply be set to rights, for everyone's heart and conscience would guide him."

Surely, any man who is faced by a choice of ways in which to act can figure out how the Golden Rule pertains to his situation. Surely, he can imagine himself in the other fellow's shoes — which is what the Golden Rule is all about — and then act rightly.

CARRY A LITTERBAG THROUGH LIFE

THE PHILOSOPHERS and poets are always telling us that life is just a road, along which we go merrily or toil patiently, occasionally coming to forks we must choose between or obstacles we must surmount.

Well, life does seem like a road. We would like to add that, as a man goes down that road, he may or may not be a litterbug. And the ugly litter that he leaves along the roadside of his life is made up of the things he should have done but didn't do. Here a scrap, there a crumpled heap — the waste of neglected deeds that he carelessly dropped. Here an insult left unsoothed, there a promise unkept, here a task not finished, there a slight left unforgiven. Unfortunately, too many of us get near the end of the trip before we think back on the mess we've left, and then we're remorseful.

Instead, though, each of us could carry a litterbag on the journey. And just as the traveler crumples up a cigarette package or candy wrapper and deposits it neatly in the bag, so does the good-living man clean up and square up his obligations as they occur. Then he can go unencumbered along the road, alert to the future and knowing that his road is clean behind him.

UP THE OPTIMISTS

OPTIMISTS are not especially in fashion these days. People tend to sneer at them and make jokes about them. For example, "An optimist is somebody who tells you to cheer up when things are going his way." Or, "A pessimist is someone who has been forced to live with an optimist."

So, optimism is taken with a grain of salt nowadays. Non-optimists figure that an optimist is somebody who doesn't know what's going on.

Well, it is a worldly world, certainly. And we've all spent a lot of time waiting for it to get as good as the optimists say it's going to get. So it isn't always easy to believe the optimists.

But, at the risk of being called naive, we're going to go right on believing them. We just can't help it. We've seen plenty of ups and downs, certainly. But it seems, when we tally them, that the ups do seem to outnumber the downs — just a little. Generally, the good days seem to outweigh the bad days. All in all, we rather approve of this world, and we're more glad than sorry that God placed us on it.

Furthermore, we think the reason the pessimists are disappointed all the time is that they usually just *wait* to see the optimists proved wrong. They say, "We're waiting, optimists. Why isn't the world getting better?" And the reason it doesn't seem to be getting better for them is just that: they're *waiting* — and waiting doesn't accomplish anything.

THE EVENING NEWS

EVENING gathers darkly around the house. The lights go on and off in the children's room, then finally stay off. Traffic noise on the street outside subsides, and the dishwasher and the vacuum cleaner are at last silent. For a few minutes, all is quiet and restful. But only for a few minutes, because soon it is time to turn on the evening news.

We Americans seem to watch the evening news as a form of self-punishment. A moment ago, everything was settled, calm, and secure in the house and the neighborhood — seemingly in all the world. But now we turn on the evening news and learn differently.

The chatter of teletypes announces that it's mayhem time.

Now we watch the luminous blue screen and listen hopelessly as the newscasters try to tell us what a panicky, hell-bent world we're living in. Back and forth across the screen flash rampaging revolutionaries, bomb blasts, running infantrymen, auto wrecks, burning buildings, strafing planes, toppling governments, riot police, injured athletes, kidnapped debutantes, political assassinations, club-wielding policemen, ambulances, sinking ships, landslides, and so forth and so on.

With their voices at doomsday pitch, the announcers try to cram all the day's chaos into fifteen minutes (not counting twelve-and-a-half minutes of commercials) . . . and then bid us a cheerful good night and invite us to tune in again tomorrow night. And so we switch off the lights and once again the quiet, safe night envelops us.

Well, at that point we ought to think — and some of us do — that probably the most significant thing the announcers have said is, "We'll see you tomorrow night." This implies that the world will still be here tomorrow in spite of all we've just heard. God, as it's been said, is quiet — but He's busy.

SO YE SHALL REAP

OUR ANCESTORS were mainly an agricultural people. At certain times each year they prepared the ground and seeded it, and prayed that God with His weather would be kind, that in a later season there would be plenty to harvest.

The times were not always kind, though, and there were droughts and untimely frosts, locust plagues and floods, famine years, and terrible burdens of work. But those people knew, down in their very bones, one great truth: whatever the future is to bring will be the harvest of what we sow now.

Because they knew that, they invested their muscles, their sweat, their intelligence and intuition, into future seasons. They worked and they waited and prayed. They worked as if the future depended on them and prayed as if the future depended on God. It might be said that they had a plain, understandable agreement among three parties: themselves, Mother Earth, and the Lord. Without that agreement, they might not have had the patience and courage to face one such hard day after another.

Days of work may be easier in our time, but not so simple as they were in the time of our forebears. Our jobs are tied into the great, complex economic system like parts in a clock. And as a clock ticks off one day at a time, every day much like every other day, just so do most of us live our lives; one day at a time, one day one task, the next day the same task repeated. Some persons say their jobs in our economic system make them feel like moving parts in a machine that never rests. And many do not really understand just how the great economic machine works, so their jobs are still more bewildering, still more pointless.

This, then, is the agony of the modern working man. It is hard for him to comprehend what his harvest is going to be. He cannot go out into the fields of earth he has planted, stand under the sun, watch the sprouts appear from the soil in spring, see the green stalks wave in the breeze in summer, or knock the golden grains off into a basket at harvest time, thanking God for His beneficence. The toil was harder then, but a man could understand the arrangement; he was securely placed between a wise God and a bountiful earth, and that was it.

The modern working man, however, is paid for his labors by lifeless, abstract tokens. He must take his harvest is such forms as money (of which there is never enough to suit him), titles and positions, stock options, fringe benefits, and retirement plans. He wants these things, of course. But what man ever falls to his knees with tears of joy in his eyes and devotion in his heart, and runs his paychecks, social security card and health policy through his fingers, whispering fervently, "Lord, I thank Thee for this Thy bounty?"

No. A man's harvest must be something rich and profoundly rewarding to his soul. There is a difference between pay and fulfillment. A man still ought to be able to know deep down in his bones that *whatever the future is to bring will be the harvest of what he sows now.*

Therefore, let him sow the seeds of compassion, gentleness,

If the law compelled them to go one mile and they went but one mile, they would feel subservient. But they could legally and proudly go beyond the law (and incidentally discomfit the Roman) by going that extra mile.

Actually, the "extra mile" principle applies very well to just about any human activity — human relations, commerce, citizenship, work. In business, for example, the businessman is required by law to do certain things — honest labeling, true weight and measure — and the law of competition compels him to treat his customers at least as fairly as does his competitor. But the enterprise that succeeds best is the one that goes beyond those laws, giving not only the merchandise, but courtesy, helpfulness, and eagerness. Likewise, the worker who does more than is required, who shows initiative and enthusiasm, succeeds best. So, too, with the friend who gives more than ordinary friendship requires, and with the mate in marriage. This is the "extra mile" principle and it is true and valid.

A TASTE OF LIFE

WE HAVE learned that the taste buds in the human tongue are specialized, the ones near the tip tasting sweetness and the ones farther back tasting bitterness.

When you pause to think about it, life in a way is like that. It starts out in the sweetness of youth and often develops through the bitterness of experience as years wear on. Many of the big and little events in life, too, progress this way. A young man's ambition or a young woman's dreams start out like a drop of honey on the tip of the tongue; then disappointments change the taste to bitterness. Many marriages start out with that sweet time appropriately called the honeymoon, then go sour. Ideals are sweet, their failure is bitter. We are as eager to have new things as a child is to have candies, then we grow dissatisfied with them as a child grows sick from too many sweets.

All these parallels are facts of life — but wait; they are not meant to be discouraging.

Think of it this way: if you have swallowed a bonbon and it is no longer sweet to your tonguetip, you do not swear off eating bonbons; instead, you anticipate the sweetness of the next one. The tongue remembers the first sweetness, rather than the bitter aftertaste, and just so the spirit remembers the sweetness of ambitions and ideals and dreams, rather than the failures, disappointments, and disillusionments.

Thus the person with a real taste for life is the person who may have had many tastes of life and always comes back to see what more good things there are.

Taste also changes: what was sweet for the youth may not be sweet for the elder. The youth's confection may have been passionate romance; the elder's, reflection and contentment; sweet to the youth was his arrogant faith in himself but sweet to the elder is his humble faith in God. Sweet to the youth may be prestigious and flashy new friends, but sweet to the elder are those comfortable old friendships that have proven lasting. Sweet to honeymooners may be new ways to kiss; sweet to Golden Anniversary celebrants are the depths of their understandings and the duration of their love.

Certainly living can be like tasting — sweet first and sour later. But, as we eat not only for the taste but for the nourishment, so do we live not only to savor but also to grow.

And growth is wisdom — a delicacy even better than sweets.

CHAPTER X
WORK

PRIORITY PRAYER FOR THE OFFICE

LORD, give me strength to postpone the things I'd rather do until the things I have to do are done! Stay my feet from wandering to the coffee wagon until my morning mail is answered. Prod me from dawdling in the hall and talking of books or health or weather when I should instead be making my appointments. Lord, lash me with the whistling whip of conscience when I sit and talk too long with idle people at lunch.

Lord, put Thy brawny Hand on the back of my swivel chair and spin me away from the window out which I tend to dreamily gaze; point me at my typewriter and then lean on me until I start to produce. Hide my fingernail clippers and pipe cleaners in deep recesses of my desk where they will not tempt my hands. Whack me smartly from behind when Thou findest me doodling. And when my thoughts are trifling, hide from me my memo pad.

Protect me from my telephone, O Lord, and challenge the joke-tellers and raconteurs who approach my office door.

I have so many things to do, Lord. With Thine infinite powers needle me to get them done, and with Thine infinite wisdom counsel me to do them honestly and forthrightly. And then when the clock announces five, I will be done. And Thy will likewise will be done.

Amen.

THE ILLUSION OF EASE

ONE of the best trademarks of a real professional, in almost any field of work, is that he makes whatever he does look so easy.

A writer tells in a book less than 130 pages long a story about a fisherman and a marlin — in language so deceptively simple that it makes most aspiring writers think, "Now, why couldn't I have written that myself?" Yet that book, *The Old Man and the Sea*, was the cap of the late Ernest Hemingway's career and was largely responsible for his winning the Nobel Prize for literature.

A good doctor talks casually to a patient while applying a few touches and instruments here and there, and then comes out with an accurate disgnosis almost before the patient realizes that an examination has been completed.

A speaker gets up before an audience and, in five minutes of conversational discourse, convinces them of something. A salesman, in the same way, breaks down someone's doubts and sales resistance and gets a signature on the dotted ling. A mechanic casually goes under the hood of a balky car and fiddles with a few tools and very shortly has it humming.

This apparent simplicity, however, is deceptive. Hemingway's clear, brief style was developed through thousands of hours of critical observation, exposure to intense experiences, rewriting and polishing for weeks on end, and agonizing self-criticism — in short, work, work and rework. The doctor's knowing ability is the result of years of excruciating study and practice. The convincing speaker may have no script before him on the podium, but he doubtless has spent hours researching facts getting his material written, and then spending additional hours practicing it before a mirror or with a tape recorder.

The crack salesman has not only studied his product and his company exhaustively, but also the needs and the very personality of his prospective customer. Perhaps he has even spent several hours just in arranging to visit that prospect at precisely the right moment. And the good mechanic has devoted himself to the understanding of motors and electrical systems; he has trained his ears and eyes and hands to recognize every symptom of malfunction.

In other words, real adeptness, of the kind that makes the hardest jobs look easy, does not just happen. Many hours, much practice, and total concentration have to be invested to create that illusion of ease.

Anyone who takes it easy in trying to attain that ease is going to have a real grind in the execution. To try to seem professional without expending the hard, disciplined effort beforehand is like trying to build a beautiful stone spire on a foundation of sand.

WHAT WORK IS ALL ABOUT

ONE OF the worst misconceptions in life is that work is a burden. Because of their resentment toward work, millions of human beings entirely miss one of life's greatest rewards.

Suppose for a moment that one full generation could be reared and educated *without* ever being told that work is to be shirked, that idleness is a neat trick to turn, that labor is one of life's miserable conditions.

Instead, suppose that one generation grew up and reared its children under the idea that work is one of the best objectives in life. That industry and creativity and productiveness are joys within themselves. That the making of a wheel or the performance of a service is a form of self-expression. And suppose that whole generation could be brought to believe the words of the poet: "When you work, you are a flute through whose heart the whispering of the hours turns to music."

Conceivably, that generation would change the soul of mankind. No longer would workers trade eight hours in indifferent effort for one day's sustenance; no longer would the factory or the office or the field be a dismal market for that trade. No longer would workers have a suspicious misunderstanding of managers, or managers a disinterest toward workers. Each would understand the other's desire to do well whatever he is supposed to do. There would be no satisfaction in getting away with an hour's loafing.

Work is necessary for man's survival, true. But it is not true that every necessity is evil. A day without some kind of constructive effort is a meaningless day.

The miracle of creation equipped us with heads, hands, and muscles which are more marvelous tools than any electronic computer, lathe, or harvesting machine. Indeed, the computer and the lathe and harvester exist only because of these natural tools were used to create them. They are monuments to the creative desire.

Man has an inherent drive to work productively. It has been through cynical maxims and slovenly thoughts that he has taught himself laziness. *Because of the old, basic nature of man, work is active innocence, and idleness is passive guilt.*

MAKING MISTAKES

"I SAW a man last week who has not made a mistake for four thousand years," wrote Herman L. Wayland. This man, Wayland went on to explain, was an Egyptian mummy in a musuem. The point Wayland was making is that no living man gets by without making mistakes. If you know someone who seems to make no mistakes, either he covers them up skillfully or he just never does anything at all. Mistakes are the learn-by-doing lessons in the school of experience. If a man makes a mistake there's no shame in that. Only if he continues in it, as Cicero the Roman statesman said, is he a fool.

Often, in fact, a lesson of life simply cannot be driven home except by the impact of a painful mistake. James Froude, the English historian, once said that "the Providence that watches over the affairs of men works out their mistakes, at times, to a healthier issue than could have been accomplished by their wisest forethought." And if anybody should know that, a historian should, history being as it is a continuing record of great mistakes and their aftermath.

When one makes a mistake, one should look back on it only long enough to infer its lesson, and then look forward, that much the wiser. Or when one finds someone else making a mistake, he should not scorn but be glad that some lesson probably has been learned. The man who admits his mistakes, corrects them, and is educated by them, is as admirable as a man would be who made no mistakes at all — if, indeed, there could exist such a man.

Thomas A. Edison, the great American inventor, did so many things right that it's not customary to think of him as a maker of mistakes. And yet, his record of mistakes, he was quick to admit, was monumental. He laid claim to having 50,000 failures in experimenting with a new storage battery alone before he got it right.

"But," Edison said, "I know fifty thousand things that won't work."

THE ESSENCE OF THINGS

THE biographer of Ernest Hemingway, A. E. Hotchner, once went to the Prado, Spain's primary art museum, with Hemingway and was puzzled at the novelist's unusual manner of visiting a gallery. Instead of making a day of it and wandering from one room to the next looking at all the pictures, Hemingway would make a special trip to the Prado and walk through the museum without looking left or right until he came to the one painting he had decided to look at that day. Then he would stay until closing time studying that one painting.

He explained later to Hotchner that what he looked for in studying a masterpiece was its essence — that one central thing that the painter was trying to express. He knew that each painter was trying to do that, Hemingway said, because in his own art, writing, every story or novel was formed around just such an essence, just such a central thought.

While this may not be everybody's preferred way of looking at a picture, there is something to be said for applying the "essence" idea to one's own life and work. For example, if a worker keeps his mind on the essential idea of the quality of his product or his service, then all the movements he makes in producing it will focus on quality. And when something is done this way, it almost invariably will result in quality. By contrast the shabbiness

85

and inferiority that are evident in so many of today's products can be traced back to workers or supervisors who are not infected with the essential idea of quality.

And so it is with life itself. A man who has chosen an essential purpose and sticks with it has good chances of living a life worthy of notice — whether it is the idea of being the best leader or the best thinker or simply the best man possible.

THE CHALLENGES OF THE TOUGH JOB

THE MAN is lucky whose job is just a little too tough for comfort; if it's too easy he won't be challenged by it. The human spirit delights in accomplishing things which at first looked almost impossible. That is why men build ever higher and ever more daring structures, why they always try to surpass the standing records in sports, why they try always to probe deeper with their literature and their science, why they try to go farther and faster into space. Man loves challenges because they give him his chance to prove his ability.

But a man does not have to be an architect or an athlete, a writer or scientist, or a space explorer to meet and surmount challenges. He needs only to have a job of work in which he can set his goals of performance a little higher every day. He can take on just a little tougher project, strive for a greater degree of perfection, and produce a greater quantity than he would have thought possible yesterday.

And in so doing, he will improve his capabilities and keep himself young and eager at heart — not through ease but through effort. There is an old saying about this: "Be thankful if your job is not quite easy; a razor cannot be sharpened on velvet."

86

A REAL ARTIST

ONCE, stopping at a diner for breakfast in a dreary section of a city, we began to take note of the short-order cook. One could not help becoming quite aware of him because of his extraordinary cheerfulness and efficiency.

He was a nondescript sort of fellow, of medium stature, with dark hair and a plain, middle-aged face — a little large in the nose, a little weak in the chin. He wore his starched white cook's cap straight as a lid, without even a rakish tilt to hint at his personality. One would not have noticed him on first glance — unless one saw him in action.

With his back turned to the counter and both hands moving swiftly over the blackened grill, reaching surely here and there in the stainless steel cabinets, flipping eggs over with deft turnings of the skillet, applying just enough butter for two slices of toast with only a couple of movements of the hand, he was preparing breakfasts for the customers of the crowded diner as fast as the waitress could call them out to him — sometimes even getting ahead of her and delivering the plates to the tables himself. He was busy but not hurried, cheerful but not effusive. In his face there was some kind of pleasant concentration.

We were glad to hear someone tell him, "I've been watching you work, and you're a true artist," because we had been intending to say the same thing to him. The cook merely gave a slight smile, neither modest nor flattered, and replied, "It's not my best day. I can't seem to get started."

We pondered about him. His was no enviable job. Perhaps he had been a short-order cook for much of his life and perhaps he might always be. Perhaps he had other ambitions and a secret dream, or perhaps he thought no further ahead than to next Saturday night when he might reward himself by drinking a little or watching a ball game. One never knows what goes on within strangers, and it is difficult sometimes even to bear in mind that something is happening within them.

Perhaps that short-order cook was quite content to be a short-order cook. It was certainly not a fascinating occupation. It would seem to be monotonous, and some would consider it menial. How could one bear to report to work morning after morning after morning in that dismal little diner? What keeps a man going at it? Mere money would not seem to be enough — and that cook certainly was not hauling down a fortune.

It is a kind of perennial question about human purposes. Sometimes any of us can stop and take a clear look at whatever we're doing, and then realize what silly activity it all is. Eight hours a day or more we perform some activity which we may or may not be truly proficient at — a third of our lifetimes — knowing all the while that we are unlikely to change the world by it. What keeps any of us going? Not just short-order cooks or janitors or stock clerks, but anybody?

We don't know. In some cases it is mere necessity. Survival. But we were able to conclude one thing — an important thing — from watching that cook work. However monotonous or menial the work, he was doing it well. And by virtue of that, he seemed more content and worthy than many seemingly successful merchants, lawyers, doctors, and bankers we've known. Perhaps once in a while some breakfasting customer watches him until moved to say, "You're a true artist at that, do you know it?"

Probably that's one of the things that keeps him going.